Teach us to Pray

Biblical Curriculum on Prayer

PRAYERFUL
PUBLISHING

Student Personal Study Guide
Transcendent Kingdom

TEACH US TO PRAY
Student Personal Study Guide

Copyright © 2019 Dale Roy Erickson

ISBN 978-0-9884145-9-4
All Rights Reserved
Published by Prayerful Publishing, Inc., Meridian, Idaho, USA
www.prayerfulpublishing.com

Cover page photos and some internal photos are provided by and used with the permission of Blair Turner. You can view more of his exceptional work at www.baravisuals.weebly.com.

Prayerful Publishing, Inc. is a non-profit 501(c)(3) ministry dedicated to providing contemporary Biblical tools on the Christian discipline of prayer for the next generation.

Teach us to Pray

Acknowledgements

To the only true God and His Son, Jesus, who brings us grace, forgiveness and life; Connie Erickson, who has stood with me through all of life's adventures; Larry Patrick for his friendship, insight, encouragement and creative graphic design; Blair Turner for his terrific pictures used on the covers and throughout the books; Errol Lester for his magnificent narration; Jim Peterson for his meticulous audio mix of the MP3 files; the Prayerful Publishing Board of Directors for their prayers, wisdom and support; Orval Mauldin for his gracious and painstaking editing; and to the host of people who challenged us to keep pressing on to the finish line. It's not over yet, and the best is yet to come.

Preface

The **Teach Us To Pray** curriculum is structured upon the various elements of prayer found in the *Lord's Prayer*. This Student Personal Study Guide is part of a multi-platform curriculum designed to help young people grow in their connection with God. The 35-lesson curriculum includes 35 short stories, a PDF handbook page that provides seven thoughts on prayer with the supporting Scripture for each lesson (a total of 245 prompts), this active participation Student Personal Study Guide, a Teacher's Manual with guidelines for teaching the lessons, a session planning sheet for each lesson, additional teacher resources, and of course, tests for each unit.

The curriculum is designed for the following possible settings: release time courses for public schools, middle school and high school youth groups, home school, Christian schools, and the training of indigenous Christian leaders.

About the Author

Dale Roy Erickson understands and lives out the importance of prayer in his individual life and in the corporate life of the church. He is established as a gifted and creative teacher who carefully studies and presents the truth of God's Word. Pastor Dale has had successful involvement in every facet of church ministry in the United States and Canada including children's, youth, adult, small group, and counseling. He has served on the national Christian education committee of the Christian & Missionary Alliance in Canada and traveled extensively across the Unites States as a field service representative specializing in youth and Christian education. He has taught release time for public high school classes for over 5 years. He serves as an example of godly living in his marriage, family, financial and personal life. It is his prayer that this curriculum will bring glory to God and provide insight for the prayer lives of many young people.

How to use this Study

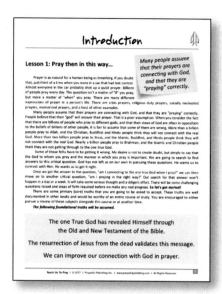

You can order these resources at www.prayerfulpublishing.com

Print or MP3

App or PDF

Print or MP3

There is a well known saying that should be changed. "Why do you believe that a small group of dedicated people can change the world? Answer: "Because it is the only thing that ever has."

Revised version: "Why do you believe that a small group of dedicated people on their knees can change the world?" Answer: "Because that is the way God chooses to work!"

Acts 1:14 They all met together continually for prayer, along with Mary the mother of Jesus, several other women, and the brothers of Jesus. NLT

Prayer Prompts Handbook Print or PDF

www.prayerfulpublishing.com

Teach us to Pray

Contents:

PRAYERFUL PUBLISHING™

Student Personal Study Guide

Teach us to Pray

A note from the Author

I would like to share a little of my heart with you before we begin this journey.

I am convinced that there is nothing of greater value than helping you connect with God.

Asaph captured my motivations quite well in **Psalm 78:1-4 NLT**

   "O my people, listen to my instructions.

(I don't want you to just listen. I want you to get involved in every way.)

   Open your ears to what I am saying, for I will speak to you in a parable.

(OK I will use YouTube videos more than parables.)

   I will teach you hidden lessons from our past – stories we have heard and known,

(I will use MP3 audio files for our stories.)

   stories our ancestors handed down to us. We will not hide these truths from our children;

(Compared to you I am ancient, but I am not one of your ancestors.)

   We will tell the next generation (presumably that's YOU) *about the glorious deeds of the Lord, about his power, and his mighty wonders."*

So I invite you to open your hearts in the hope of catching a glimpse of His glorious deeds, His power and His mighty wonders!

– Dale

Introduction

Lesson 1: Pray then in this way...

> *Many people assume that their prayers are connecting with God, and that they are "praying" correctly.*

Prayer is as natural for a human being as breathing. If you doubt that, just think of a time when you were in a car that had lost control. Almost everyone in the car probably shot up a quick prayer. Billions of people pray every day. The question isn't a matter of "if" you pray, but more a matter of "when" you pray. There are many different expressions of prayer in a person's life. There are crisis prayers, religious duty prayers, socially motivated prayers, memorized prayers, and a host of other examples.

Many people assume that their prayers are connecting with God, and that they are "praying" correctly. People believe that their "god" will answer their prayer. That is a poor assumption. When you consider the fact that there are billions of people who pray to different gods, and that their views of God are often in opposition to the beliefs of billions of other people, it is fair to assume that some of them are wrong. More than a billion people pray to Allah, and the Christian, Buddhist and Hindu people think they will not connect with the real God. More than two billion people pray to Jesus, and the Islamic, Buddhist, and Hindu people think they will not connect with the real God. Nearly a billion people pray to Brahman, and the Islamic and Christian people think they are not getting through to the one true God.

Some of these folks have to be getting it wrong. My desire is not to create doubt, but simply to say that the God to whom you pray and the manner in which you pray is important. We are going to search to find answers to this critical question. God has not left us on our own in pursuing these questions. He wants us to connect with Him. He wants us to get it right.

Once we get the answer to the question, "Am I connecting to the one true God when I pray?", we can then move on to another critical question, "Am I praying in the right way?". Our search for that answer won't happen in a day or a week. It will take some serious thought and diligent effort. There will be some challenging questions raised, and steps of faith required, before we make any real progress. **So let's get started!**

There are some primary (core) truths that you are going to be asked to accept. These truths are well documented in other books and would be worthy of an entire course of study. You are encouraged to either pursue a review of these subjects alongside this course or at another time.

The following foundational truths will be assumed:

The one True God has revealed Himself through Creation and the Old and New Testament of the Bible.

The resurrection of Jesus from the dead validates this message.

We can improve our connection with God in prayer.

Having laid the foundation for our search, it's now time dig in to discover what the Bible has to say about this thing we call "prayer." The Bible gives us some examples of people who clearly "got it right." If connecting with God had a *Hall of Fame*, these people would be found there. Some answers may require extra effort to discover the Hall of Fame character. Look up the Scripture, and give the name of the Prayer Hall of Fame character in the blank space provided.

- Prayer Hall of Fame -

I prayed all night asking God for help before picking my team.
Luke 6:12-13 _____

I saved my nephew from death by changing my prayer request five times.
Genesis 18:22-33 _____

I told the Pharisees God doesn't hear the prayer of sinners but does hear the prayers of a godly man. **John 9:24-31** _____

It was well known to my friends and enemies that I prayed three times a day.
Daniel 6:10 _____

I faced a life-threatening challenge and was part of rescuing a whole race of people after preparing myself through three days of fasting.
Esther 4:16-17 _____

I said, "If I let sin rule in my heart, God won't listen to me."
Psalms 66:18-20 _____

When I saw God I said: "I'm doomed because I'm a sinful man," but God forgave me.
Isaiah 6:5-7 _____

Jesus asked me to stay and pray with Him for one hour, but I fell asleep.
Mark 14:37-38 _____

After an all night wrestling match I asked God to bless me, and God gave me a new name.
Genesis 32:24-28 _____

Just like Jesus, I am someone who taught my disciples to pray.
Luke 11:1 _____

I wrote the Bible verse that says: "If anyone is in trouble, he should pray."
James 5:13 _____

I simply prayed these seven words: "Please heal her, O Lord, I pray." And she was healed.
Numbers 12:13 _____

When I finished a long public prayer, God sent fire into the temple and the priests had to stay out. **2 Chronicles 7:1-2** _____

I offered a praise prayer offering which is now called the Magnificat.
Luke 1:46-55 _____

I wrote the part of the Bible that says: "Pray without ceasing."
1 Thessalonians 1:1, 5:17 _____

When I prayed for friends who misrepresented God, I received a double blessing.
Job 42:10 _____

I shot up a quick and silent prayer before making a request before the king.
Nehemiah 2:2-4 _____

I prayed for a child with such fervor that the High Priest thought I was drunk.
1 Samuel 1:12-13 _____

I made a real connection with God because I went to a public place for prayer.
Acts 16:13-14 _____

After my husband died I spent nearly every day fasting and praying until the Messiah was born. **Luke 2:36-38** _____

I told the king I didn't need his protection, and then fasted and asked God to protect us.
Ezra 8:21-23 _____

I said: "It would be a sin for me to stop praying for you."
1 Samuel 12:23 _____

I said, "Don't be afraid. Those who are with us are more than those who are with them."
2 Kings 6:16-17 _____

I made it a priority to always pray that others would know the will of God.
Colossians 4:12 _____

I said, "I have sinned… because I feared the people and listened to their voice," (i.e. not God's voice). **1 Samuel 15:24** _____

The list could go on and on, but this is a good start.

It should encourage us to say as the disciples said to Jesus: *"Teach us to pray as John taught his disciples to pray."* Clearly, they believed that "prayer" was something that could be taught and learned. While prayer is truly simple enough that any child can do it, it is also significant and complex enough that we will never completely master it.

Who would you add to your Prayer Hall of Fame? This can be someone listed in the Bible, or someone you know or have heard about. List as many as possible....

_____   _____

_____   _____

_____   _____

_____   _____

- Notes -

_____

_____

_____

_____

_____

_____

_____

_____

_____

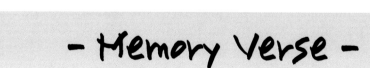

Read Lesson 1 Short Story: HHU Vol. 1 - Cathy's Camaro

- Memory Verse -

It happened that while Jesus was praying in a certain place, after He had finished, one of His disciples said to Him, "Lord, teach us to pray just as John also taught his disciples." Luke 11:1 **NASB**

Introduction

Lesson 2: Diligently search for Him

> *If we think we have to impress other people with our prayers, we are entirely missing the point.*

Connecting with God (relationship/prayer) is in some ways a paradox. As we learned at the end of our last lesson, it is so simple that any child can do it effectively. In fact, Jesus indicates that we must become like a child in order to enter His kingdom (Matthew 18:3), and that the kingdom of God (referencing children) belongs to such as these (Matthew 19:14). On the other hand, we are challenged to grow up in the faith and not be like children anymore (Ephesians 4:13-14). Some would like to make effective prayer all about the words we choose, or the emotion we bring with our prayers. Little children don't do that. They simply say what they want, and mean what they say. As we look over the various Scriptures on the matter, it becomes clear that prayer is much more a matter of our hearts than our choice of words.

Let me illustrate this by telling you the true story of a man who had a terrible stuttering problem. He had tried everything he could do to deal with the challenge. One day, while driving his car, he was pressed into praying, and his words were perfectly formed. When asked why he didn't stutter when he prayed, he simply said: "I'm letting God know what's on my heart." He stuttered because he was concerned about what others would think of his choice of words. Many of us get concerned about what others think of us. That can be especially true when we pray. We might feel free to speak out boldly about sports or politics or our family, but when it comes to prayer, we can easily become intimidated.

One cure for this would come from realizing that God already knows what's on our hearts, and that is all that really matters. If we think we have to impress other people with our prayers, we are entirely missing the point. The **audience that we are looking for is the God of the Universe**, not our friends across the room. Knowing that God is listening to what we are saying would be really intimidating if we didn't know that He loves us dearly. We come as children to a loving Father to let Him know our needs. That sounds pretty easy right? It really is, but then why do so many people seem unable to really connect? That is what today's lesson is about.

Our connection with God is all about *relationship*. All relationships have a starting place, and a good relationship will grow in depth and meaning. If a young girl gains the interest of a young boy, the first conversation may seem awkward or even uneasy. Even if both of them show some subtle interest, the first public conversation may be challenging. This will especially be true if this is the first time that either of them have had some interest in the opposite sex. Some young people will have more confidence than others, but as a general rule most will find that first encounter difficult. Once they get past the first self-conscious moments, the conversations generally get easier.

Let's go Treasure Hunting!

For this relationship to grow, each person will have to share more about their experiences, likes and dislikes, motivations, hopes and dreams. They will have to spend time together talking about these things. The same is true in our relationship with God, except in His case, the search is unfathomable. Yes, we will come to know Him as our Father, friend, protector, provider, etc. Like anything of real value, discovering all about the many facets of God will take some work. It's like searching for treasure. Colossians 2:3 says this about Jesus: *In whom are hidden all the treasures of wisdom and knowledge.*

Let's Go Treasure Hunting Together!

The Bible gives us some clues that will help us in this search for this treasure. (Unless otherwise indicated, the New American Standard Version is used... NLT = New Living Translation NKJV = New King James Version)

Deuteronomy 4:29 NLT tells us that if we search for Him with all our _____, and _____, we will find Him.

Deuteronomy 6:5 NLT tells us that we must love the Lord your God with all your _____, all your _____ and all your _____.

Matthew 22:37 Jesus said that you shall love the Lord your God with all your _____, with all your _____ and with all your _____.

Deuteronomy 10:12 NLT asks "What does the Lord your God require of you? He requires you to _____ Him, to live according to His _____, to _____ and _____ Him with all your _____ and _____."

1 Samuel 12:24 teaches us to _____ the Lord and _____ Him in _____ with all your _____. For consider what great things He has done for you.

Hebrews 11:6 tells us that without _____ it is _____ to please God, for the one who comes to God must _____ that He is and that His is the _____ of those who _____ Him.

1 Chronicles 16:10 reveals that we should _____ in His holy name; Let the _____ of those who _____ the Lord be _____.

1 Chronicles 16:11 says _____ the Lord and His strength; _____ His face _____.

Matthew 6:33 challenges us to _____ _____ His kingdom and His _____ and all these _____ will be added to you.

1 Chronicles 22:19 Now _____ your heart and your soul to seek the LORD your God;

2 Chronicles 15:12 They entered into the _____ to _____ the LORD God of their fathers with all their _____ and _____.

Psalm 9:10 And those who _____ Your name will put their _____ in You, for You, O LORD, have not _____ those who _____ You.

1 Chronicles 28:9 "As for you, my son Solomon, _____ the God of your father, and _____ Him with a _____ _____ and a _____

_____; for the LORD _____ all hearts, and understands _____ intent of the thoughts. If you _____ Him, He will let you _____ Him; but if you _____ Him, He will _____ you forever.

Colossians 3:1-2 Therefore if you have been raised up with Christ, _____ _____ the things above, where Christ is, seated at the right hand of God. _____ your mind on the things _____, not on the things that are on _____.

Mark 12:30 AND YOU SHALL LOVE THE LORD YOUR GOD WITH ALL YOUR _____, AND WITH ALL YOUR _____, AND WITH ALL YOUR _____, AND WITH ALL YOUR _____.

Psalm 34:4 I _____ the LORD, and He _____ me, and delivered me from all my _____.

Psalm 34:10 The young lions do lack and suffer hunger; but they who _____ the LORD shall not be in want of any _____ thing.

Psalm 105:4 _____ the LORD and His strength; seek His face _____.

Acts 8:36-37 As they went along the road they came to some water; and the eunuch said, "Look! Water! What prevents me from being baptized ?" And Philip said, "If you _____ with all your _____, you may." And he answered and said, "I believe that Jesus Christ is the Son of God."

Proverbs 8:17 "I love those who _____ me; and those who _____ seek me will find me."

Isaiah 55:6 _____ the LORD while He may be _____; _____ upon Him while He is _____.

Isaiah 33:6 And He will be the _____ of your times, a wealth of salvation, _____ and knowledge; the fear of the LORD is his _____.

Hebrews 7:19 (for the Law made nothing perfect), and on the other hand there is a bringing in of a _____ hope, through which we _____ _____ to God.

Luke 10:27 And he answered, "YOU SHALL _____ THE LORD YOUR GOD WITH _____ YOUR _____, AND WITH ALL YOUR _____, AND WITH ALL YOUR _____, AND WITH ALL YOUR _____; AND YOUR _____ AS YOURSELF."

Jeremiah 29:13 You will _____ Me and _____ Me when you search for Me with _____ _____ _____.

Amos 5:4 For thus says the LORD to the house of Israel, "_____ Me that you may _____."

Daniel 9:3 So I gave my attention to the Lord God to seek Him by _____ and _____, with _____, sackcloth and ashes.

Zechariah 8:21 NKJV The inhabitants of one city shall go to another, saying, "Let us continue to go and _____ before the Lord, and _____ the Lord of hosts. I myself will _____ also."

Matthew 6:20-21 "But store up for yourselves _____ in heaven, where neither moth nor rust destroys, and where thieves do not break in or steal; for where your _____ is, there your _____ will be also."

Romans 11:33 Oh, the _____ of the riches both of the wisdom and knowledge of God! How _____ are His judgments and _____ His ways!

Have you ever lost something that was really important to you? How did you feel when you were searching for it? _____

_____

_____

Describe how you felt when you were unable to find it. _____

_____

_____

Have you ever found something of great value? How did that make you feel? _____

_____

_____

Read Lesson 2 Short Story: HHU Vol. 1 - Triggers

- Memory Verse -

And he answered, "YOU SHALL LOVE THE LORD YOUR GOD WITH ALL YOUR HEART, AND WITH ALL YOUR SOUL, AND WITH ALL YOUR STRENGTH, AND WITH ALL YOUR MIND; AND YOUR NEIGHBOR AS YOURSELF." Luke 10:27 **NASB**

Lesson 3: Creator of heaven and earth

> *"How did we get here, and what does that tell us about the meaning of our lives?"*

The Bible starts with these words: *In the beginning God*. Which God? What was He like? Keep reading and He will tell you all about Himself, but let's be clear: there's no point reading any further if you don't believe the first four words! *In the beginning God*. You must believe that He is... that He exists. It's going to take faith because you weren't there in the beginning. None of us were. Hebrews 11:6 says: "But without faith it is impossible to please Him, for he who comes to God must believe that He is, and that He is a rewarder of those who diligently seek Him."

This is called *the first premise*. The starting point of your reasoning and/or argument will lead towards or away from certain conclusions. If we start our belief system with the first premise of the Bible... i.e., in the beginning God... then everything that follows will be possible. If we start our belief system with the first premise, "there is no God," then we are led to a different set of outcomes. Either way, we are led to a "faith decision" because neither premise can be proven... at least not by direct observation or scientific evidence.

We can pursue different kinds of evidence in order to make our "faith decision." We can study people and try to determine what their "behaviors or belief systems" produce. That is just a fancy way of asking: "What seems to work well for the long term in real life?" **We can use scientific evidence as a benchmark, but that will have its limits. Scientific evidence can only allow that which can be measured and repeated.**

We can utilize historical evidence in support of our faith decision. We can investigate philosophical theories, religious belief systems, anthropological treatises, and a host of other potential sources to support our faith decision. At the end of our search, we ultimately must answer these questions: *"How did we get here, and what does that tell us about the meaning of our lives?"* The Bible addresses these questions quickly and clearly... *In the beginning God*.

Once we have ceded that point, we have the proper foundation for a relationship with God. Scripture quickly answers our next big question: "How did we get here?" In the first three chapters of the Bible we are told: "In the beginning God created the heavens and the earth."

As God reveals more of the story, we find out where we stand with Him and why. We learn how to approach an infinite God who is clearly beyond our finite (limited to space and time) comprehension.

That is essentially what this course is all about.

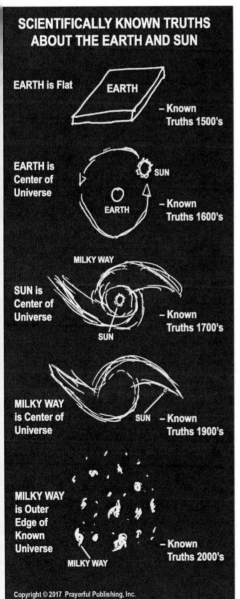

SCIENTIFICALLY KNOWN TRUTHS ABOUT THE EARTH AND SUN

EARTH is Flat — Known Truths 1500's

EARTH is Center of Universe — Known Truths 1600's

SUN is Center of Universe — Known Truths 1700's

MILKY WAY is Center of Universe — Known Truths 1900's

MILKY WAY is Outer Edge of Known Universe — Known Truths 2000's

Copyright © 2017 Prayerful Publishing, Inc.

http://en.wikipedia.org/wiki/History_of_the_Center_of_the_Universe
Illustration courtesy Chris Erickson

If we accept the next six words, "created the heavens and the earth," immediately following the first four "In the beginning God," we know "how we got here." We can then begin to pursue: "What does that tell us about the meaning of our lives?" The created being must go to the Creator to discover the "why?" of its existence. For example: if we hope to know the purpose for a particular bridge, we would have to consult with the architect and engineers. Before I will drive across that bridge, I would like more evidence than: "there was a huge gas/matter explosion somewhere in space and time," and the bridge just appeared. That's not an answer that most people will accept when making their "faith decision." Don't tell your science teacher, but the vast majority of people in the world would say, "There is a God and *He created the heavens and the earth.*"

The implications of accepting the truth that there is a God and He is the creator has many ramifications in a person's life. The outcomes are set forth in the first chapter of the book of Romans. Some of the natural consequences are not always widely accepted by the general public, but our goal is to see what the Bible might have to say on these issues.

- Two Paths -

There are 10 statements/values/opinions listed in the chart below. Read Romans 1:16-32 and then place a check mark to the right of the column that best represents whether the statement flows from the view that God DID or DID NOT create the heavens and the earth.

	God DID create the heavens and the earth	✓	God DID NOT create the heavens and the earth	✓
1	Popular opinion defines what is right behavior		Popular opinion defines what is right behavior	
2	Animals are worthy of being worshipped		Animals are worthy of being worshipped	
3	Passion decides the proper "expression" of love		Passion decides the proper "expression" of love	
4	The universe provides evidence of God's existence		The universe provides evidence of God's existence	
5	God defines what is TRUE (truth is absolute)		God defines what is TRUE (truth is absolute)	
6	Government defines which actions are evil		Government defines which actions are evil	
7	Each person defines what is TRUE (truth is relative)		Each person defines what is TRUE (truth is relative)	
8	People who deny God's existence are fools		People who deny God's existence are fools	
9	Wrong beliefs about God lead to unnatural passion		Wrong beliefs about God lead to unnatural passion	
10	Living the good life begins with a faith decision		Living the good life begins with a faith decision	

What we believe about God is critical to our relationship with Him. God has revealed Himself not merely as *the Creator*. While our first steps to knowing God begin with believing that He is who He says He is, there is a lot more to learn after we accept that truth. He designed us for *relationship with Him.*

God is **holy**, which impacts how we must approach him. God is **love**, which defines how He chooses to relate to us. And He is **perfect** in all His ways, which tells us that we can trust Him. *Let's keep digging. God will help us find our way!*

- Notes -

_____
_____
_____
_____
_____
_____
_____
_____
_____
_____
_____
_____
_____
_____
_____
_____
_____
_____

Read Lesson 3 Short Story: HHU Vol. 1 - New Job

- Memory Verse -

For by Him all things were created, both in the heavens and on earth, visible and invisible, whether thrones or dominions or rulers or authorities — all things have been created through Him and for Him. Colossians 1:16 **NASB**

Approach with Awe

Lesson 4: The God of Holiness

*...approach with caution because "**this is holy ground.**"*

A failure to show respect for a person's name is a failure to respect the person. In the world that I grew up in "respect had to be earned," but even when earned it wasn't always granted. I was taught to respect certain positions in life. I was told that we must respect our parents, teachers, military personnel, pastors, police officers and government officials. The list was long, and sometimes undeserved. To make things even more complicated, there were different kinds of respect. Some, like the school bully, were treated with respect out of fear. Mothers might gain respect through acts of kindness and compassion. The tales of clergy misconduct worked their way into the "respect your authorities" mosaic. Some teachers gained respect by challenging our intellect, while others lost respect through careless behavior. Perceived integrity, followed by undeniable dishonesty, became a narrative about government officials. With the passing of time, only the naive granted untested thoughts of respect. Sounds like a pretty bleak outlook for the concept of respecting authority. Where does a person go when every human agency has failed in some way to garner respect?

Perhaps this is where Moses found himself as he wandered in the desert near Mount Horeb. Moses' life was not perfect in Midian, but at least he was out from under the tyrannical rule of the Pharaoh. He would stuff

http://mediaprocessor.websimages.com/width/277/crop/0,0,277x164/
www.jstokeswritingministries.com/Burning-Bush-610x351-1.jpg

his memories of the Hebrew enslavement and his murderous act. He was clearly justified in what he did, right? The problem Moses didn't anticipate was that God was watching. The Hebrew slaves were crying out for help and Moses was unaware that he was going to be a part of God's solution.

In a moment, everything in his life was changed. He sees an unbelievable sight. He sees a bush that is burning, but isn't being consumed. Intrigue becomes fear, which is quickly transformed into reverence. God invites him to show his respect by taking off his shoes and then

reveals Himself by telling Moses His name. God makes it clear from the start that he must show reverence for His name. Later, He is even more clear when He says: *"You shall not take the name of the Lord your God in vain, for the Lord will not leave him unpunished who takes His name in vain."* If God is that concerned about "His Name," perhaps we should take a closer look.

That's what Moses did.

*I'm warning you… approach with caution because "**this is holy ground**."*

– The Names of God –

We can gain a more complete understanding of how to relate to God from the names that He has chosen for Himself. Exodus chapter three is a good example of this. **Review some of the Names of God in the table below and find verses in Exodus 3:1-22 that illustrate God acting in a manner that is consistent with His Name. Place the verse and phrase that reveals His nature in the adjacent columns in the table. There may be more than one correct answer.**

Name of God revealing His nature/attribute	Verse #	Exodus 3 phrase that illustrates God's nature
Yahweh - God of purity, perfection i.e. hollness		
Yahweh Elohim - personal God... of your father...		
El Ro'i - God who sees what is happening in our lives		
El Shaddai - The Almighty... all powerful God		
Jehovah Ro'i - The God who is my shepherd		
Adonai - The God who is our Lord and Master		
Jehovah Shammah - The God who is with us		
El Olam - The God who is eternal		
Jehovah Jireh - The God who provides for us		
El Elyon - Most High God, the God over all gods		
Jehovah Tsidkenu - The God of righteousness		

God tells Moses His name, and then sends him on a mission to demonstrate who He is to the people of Israel who are languishing in Egypt. Moses says that he isn't up to the task. A summary of God's response seems to be: *"Don't worry about it... I've got this."* In Exodus 3:20 He tells Moses "so *I* will stretch out *My* hand and strike Egypt with all *My* wonders which *I* will do in its midst; and after that he will let you go." Exodus 12:12 and Numbers 33:4 indicate that the 10 plagues were judgments on the gods of Egypt. The plagues demonstrated that the God of Israel is the one true God, and that He was more powerful than the "gods" that the Egyptians worshipped.

Generations come and go, and yet the fear of inadequacy remains the same. Moses is not alone in these feelings. Gideon said that his family's position among the people of Israel disqualified him. Paul said, "I didn't come to Corinth with superiority of speech or wisdom... but was among you in weakness and in fear and in much trembling... so that your faith would not rest in the wisdom of men, but on the power of God."

Let's explore this further by looking at how God demonstrated His judgments specifically against the Egyptians gods.

Khnum, an ancient Egyptian ram-headed god who creates people and their kas on his potter's wheel. Based on New Kingdom tomb paintings.

By Montu.svg: [1] (Own work derivative work: Insider (talk)) [CC BY-SA 3.0 via Wikimedia Commons

– Matching Exercise –

Identify the description of the "gods" that the Egyptians worshipped and the corresponding plague that the Egyptians encountered. You can find the plagues listed in Exodus chapters 7-11.

1____ **Khnum** - Guardian of the Nile.
Egyptians believed that waters of the Nile River brought them life.

A) Livestock disease

2____ **Heqt** - Egyptian goddess of birth and wife of the creator of the world. She was represented as a frog.

B) Frogs

3____ **Geb** - Egyptian god representing the creator of the earth.
Any impurity on the body of a priest prevented them from performing any priestly duties.

C) Locusts

4____ **Khepri** - Egyptian creator of gods and kings.
It was represented with the head of a scarab beetle.

D) Darkness

5____ **Apis** - The Apis Bull was said to hold the power of prophecy.

E) Death of the Firstborn

6____ **Serapis** - The god of healing.
Imhotep - The god of medicine.

F) Boils

7____ **Isis** and **Seth** were charged with the protection of the crops.
The burned fields would have been a testimony to their impotence.

G) Swarms of scarab beetles

8____ **Nepri** - The god of grain.
Ermutet & Thermuthis - The gods of childbirth, crops, fertility and harvest.

H) Lice

9____ **Amon-Ra** - Represented by a man's body and a falcon's head surmounted with a solar disk (sun god).

I) Nile turned to blood

10____ **Isis** - The goddess of fertility.
Selket - The guardian of life.
Min - The god of procreation.
Renenutet - The guardian of Pharaoh.

J) Hail

The New Covenant reveals many more facets of the nature of our God. They are entirely consistent with the names of God which we have reviewed as found in the Old Covenant. Hebrews 12:28-29 tells us that our God is a consuming fire who must be approached with reverence. Colossians 1:16 reveals Jesus as the Creator God who holds all things together and has authority over every position of power in heaven and earth. 1 Peter 1:15-17 challenges us: "but as He who called you is holy, you also be holy in all your conduct, because it is written, 'Be holy, for I am holy.' And if you call on the Father, who without partiality judges according to each one's work, conduct yourselves throughout the time of your stay here in fear". Matthew 5:48 defines that even more carefully by instructing us "therefore you shall be perfect, just as your Father in heaven is perfect."

I remember the first time I read that verse and I cried out to God "I can't… I've tried and I just can't be perfect!" I struggled with that verse for many years, and God finally showed me the point of that verse. He graciously let me know that He knew that I couldn't be perfect, and that I had to come to realize that truth.

per•fec•tion (pər-fĕkˈshun)

- the quality or state of being perfect
- freedom from fault or defect
- an exemplification of supreme excellence
- the act or process of perfecting

https://www.merriam-webster.com/dictionary/perfection

Yes, the standard that the holiness (purity, righteousness) of God requires **is** perfection. The Bible makes it very clear in many places that there isn't a man or woman alive who can attain that standard through their own effort. What we need to do is admit it. Tell God that we can't measure up. It's called repentance… admitting that we fall short of God's standard and asking for His help in changing the direction of our lives. It's very simple – as simple as A-B-C!

Admit to God that you don't meet the standard of perfection.

Believe that Jesus' death on the cross paid the penalty for your imperfection and ask God to

Change your life.

Some people call it being born again (John 3:3), or the start of God's work of making all things new in our lives (2 Corinthians 5:17).

God has revealed that there are many facets to our relationship with Him. He is our Creator, our Savior, our Lord and Master, our Father in heaven, our Protector, our Friend, etc. We will take a look at many of these attributes of our relationship with God throughout this course. How should the fact that our God is holy impact our attitude as we come before Him in prayer?

Read Hebrews 4:16 as a starting point in our answer to that question. "Let us therefore come boldly to the throne of grace, that we may obtain mercy and find grace to help in time of need." Let the adventure begin!

Read Lesson 4 Short Story: HHU Vol. 1 - A Woman's Scream

- Memory Verse -

He made Him who knew no sin to be sin on our behalf, so that we might become the righteousness of God in Him. 2 Cor. 5:21 NIV

Approach with Awe

Lesson 5: The God of Love

Most people on this planet should have their god put out with the trash. Their god is a hand-me-down. Like some hand-me-downs, the person who had it didn't really want it in the first place. It is true that some hand-me-downs are really valuable and we are glad to get them, but that is the exception rather than the rule. When it comes to our relationship with the God of the universe, hand-me-downs just won't do. It's far too important to simply accept whatever someone else wants to give you.

That's how it usually works though. Mom and Dad's views and misconceptions about God are generally accepted without serious investigation. They probably did the same with their parents, and their parents with their parents. And so down through the generations the blessings of those who "got it right" flow like a river following the path of least resistance. Unfortunately, the curse of those who got it wrong flows just as easily down a similar path.

Generation after generation worship through some form of the Hindu, Buddhist, or Muslim religion or even a version of the Christian or Jewish faith. We have already established the fact that God will be found by the person who diligently searches for Him. We've also looked at the fact that there are different kinds of evidence. Some will be helpful and some won't.

What kind of evidence will you choose in your search? How do we even know where to look for evidence that we can trust? Here's one that everyone will have access to: genuine expressions of love. It will be a subjective source of information, but all truth will not be wrapped in an objective box with a bow on the top. Jesus actually invited the world to evaluate his followers by the standard found in John 13:35, the love that they had for one another.

What does that look like? Where does it come from? The Bible gives us many answers to those questions. A very good example of those answers can be found in 1 John 4:7-21.

Looking for LOVE in All the Right Places!

Read each verse from 1 John 4:7-21 and give your answer as to what God says about what "love" looks like and/or its source.

Verse 7: _____

_____

Verse 8: _____

_____

Verse 9: _____

_____

Verse 10: _____

_____

Verse 11: _____

_____

Verse 12: _____

_____

Verse 13: _____

_____

Verse 14: _____

_____

Verse 15: _____

_____

Verse 16: _____

_____

Verse 17: _____

_____

Verse 18: _____

_____

Verse 19: _____

_____

Verse 20: _____

_____

Verse 21: _____

_____

– I LOVE IT Exercise –

Rank the following quotes about love on a scale from 1-10.

1 = don't like at all   10 = really love it!

1. _____ As the wings of a bird in full flight, love is unable to be constrained. Regardless of the maps you try to draw for it, love knows only one path - towards the object of its passion. – *Richard Bach*

2. _____ The supreme happiness of life is the conviction that we are loved; loved for ourselves, or rather loved in spite of ourselves.   – *Victor Hugo*

3. _____ Take away love and our earth is a tomb.   – *Robert Browning*

4. _____ What the world needs now is love, sweet love; it's the only thing that there's just too little of.   – *Burt Bacharach/Hal David*

5. _____ Love is patient, love is kind and is not jealous; love does not brag and is not arrogant, does not act unbecomingly; it does not seek its own, is not provoked, does not take into account a wrong suffered, does not rejoice in unrighteousness, but rejoices with the truth, bears all things, believes all things, hopes all things, endures all things. Love never fails. – *Apostle Paul*

6. _____ If you judge people, you have no time to love them.   – *Mother Theresa*

7. _____ There is no remedy for love but to love more.   – *Henry David Thoreau*

8. _____ "Greater love has no one than this, that one lay down his life for his friends." – *Jesus Christ*

9. _____ The best and most beautiful things in this world cannot be seen or even heard, but must be felt with the heart.   – *Helen Keller*

10. _____ I love you, not only for what you are, but for what I am when I am with you. – *Roy Croft*

- Love Songs -

One of the most common ways to express our feelings about love is through a song. What is your favorite song that talks about "love"? Why would you choose that particular one?

_____
_____
_____

Have you ever seen people who are "in love"? How did you know they were in love? Describe what their love for one another looked like?

_____
_____
_____

What does God's love for you look like? What does your love for God look like?

_____
_____
_____

Reflect upon the love demonstrated in the following verses and then write a brief prayer thanking God for His love for you. (Romans 5:6-8, 8:37-39, John 3:16, Ephesians 5:1-2)

_____
_____
_____
_____
_____

Read Lesson 5 Short Story: HHU Vol. 1 - Extraordinary

- Memory Verse -

This is real love – not that we loved God, but that he loved us and sent his Son as a sacrifice to take away our sins. 1 John 4:10 NLT

Lesson 6: The God of Righteousness

Where is He when I am screaming "that's not fair!" at the top of my lungs?

Sometimes bad things happen to good people, and good things happen to bad people. Have you ever been there? You know, that person who is just a frog's hair above pond scum, and he won the lottery. The other guy was just naturally good to the core… didn't even have to work at it, and he came home from Afghanistan without his legs. That's not how it's supposed to work, but that is how it is sometimes.

Solomon said it this way in Ecclesiastes 8:14: *There is a vanity which occurs on earth, that there are just men to whom it happens according to the work of the wicked; again, there are wicked men to whom it happens according to the work of the righteous. I said that this also is vanity. On the other hand, there are evil men to whom it happens according to the deeds of the righteous.* There's something wrong here. There are a lot of injustices in this world. Some of them are just small and irritating, while others are in your face and devastating. When they happen to other people, it is pretty easy to look the other way. But when it comes our way… well now, that is a different story. Where is God in all of this? Does He accept responsibility for this whole mess? Where is He when I am screaming "That's not fair!" at the top of my lungs?

You may not have been in this situation "yet," but in time nearly everyone on the planet will be looking for the answer to those questions. You can hardly turn on the television without getting an up close and personal video view of something traumatic. We want to hold somebody responsible, and God is the first one who comes to mind. Isn't He in charge of everything? *Yes!* Is God all powerful? *Yes!* Doesn't He see everything that is happening? *Yes!* Then why doesn't He solve this problem and make it go away?

Good questions, but they overlook one very important fact of history. When God started this whole mess we call the world, it was perfect. Adam was perfect. Eve was perfect. Their world **was perfect**. Only one thing could mess up that perfect world. They only had one thing to keep right and they couldn't do it. Where was God when they messed things up? He was already making a plan to undo the mess.

WHERE IS GOD IN ALL OF THIS?

Picture your little brother or sister searching for something in your room. Clothes are strewn everywhere, important things knocked over, and something has been spilled on your computer. It looks like a tornado has hit your room. Can you picture this (even if you don't have a little brother or sister)? What are you going to do? I mean, what are you going to do after you calm down? What would you do if you knew you could get away with it? Don't answer that! Don't even think about that! When Adam and Eve messed up God's perfect world, there were consequences. There are always consequences and we are living with them now – but God has a plan! See this Lesson's Memory Verse Romans 8:28.

His plan will one day take us back to that perfect world and do it even one better. God is going *change us completely*, so that this time we can't and won't mess it up. So what does that have to do with the mess we are in right now, and the injustice you will face, or may be facing right now? That is the question we hope to address in this lesson. Let's take a look at a Bible passage that might point us in the right direction. Read **Psalm 34** and think of what would be a normal response to suffering if we believed that life on earth is all there is. What would be a normal response to a tragedy if we are eternal beings who will one day be perfect, and once again live in God's perfect world? *Those are two radically different points of view!*

– Eternal Perspective –

It is pretty easy to believe that God is good and kind and just when things go our way. The real challenge comes when they don't. **Use Psalm 34 as a gauge** of what a normal response would be if we believed that God was going to make things perfect again. When difficulties, suffering and/or injustice comes, write down what a normal response might be if we saw things from an earthly or from an eternal perspective.

Earthly Perspective   Eternal Perspective

Finite View	My life on earth is all there is.	Eternal View	My life extends beyond this earth.

A classmate calls the Christian music you listen to "garbage."

Finite beings might say this		1-3 Eternal beings might say	

The parents of your best friend are getting a divorce.

Finite beings might say this		4-7 Eternal beings might say	

One of your parents gets fired and your family is about to lose the house.

Finite beings might say this		8-10 Eternal beings might say	

A classmate lies about you by saying that you cheated on a test.

Finite beings might say this		11-14 Eternal beings might say	

A friend of your older brother is killed by a drunk driver.

Finite beings might say this		15-18 Eternal beings might say	

Your sister was in a skiing accident and is in the hospital.

Finite beings might say this		19-20 Eternal beings might say	

A teacher mocks you for being Christian.

Finite beings might say this		21-22 Eternal beings might say	

It is one thing to say that God is going to make everything perfect someday, but what about today? Why should I even try to be good if good things sometimes happen to bad people, and bad things sometimes happen to good people? It's really hard to accept the idea that what happens isn't always directly related to how good or evil you are. We've already established that we need to take an eternal perspective to God dealing with people in a just manner.

But is justice and reward only a matter of heavenly reward in the "sweet by and by"? God says otherwise. In many places God says that, as a general rule, there will be reward on the earth for righteous living. Proverbs 11 gives us some examples of the kinds of rewards that "doing what is right" will lead to.

– Righteous Expectations –

Read Proverbs chapter 11 NKJV and match the correct verse to the expectations of the righteous.

_____ Verse 3	A)	leads to life
_____ Verse 4	B)	they will flourish
_____ Verse 5	C)	will be rewarded on the earth (i.e. not just in heaven)
_____ Verse 6	D)	delivered from trouble
_____ Verse 8	E)	delivers them from lustful traps
_____ Verse 9	F)	God delights in them
_____ Verse 10-11	G)	the fruit of righteousness is a tree of life
_____ Verse 18	H)	the one who sows righteousness gets a sure reward
_____ Verse 19	I)	their descendents will be delivered
_____ Verse 20	J)	their desire is only good
_____ Verse 21	K)	integrity will guide them
_____ Verse 23	L)	delivered through knowledge
_____ Verse 28	M)	delivers them from death
_____ Verse 30	N)	city is exalted and rejoices when the righteous do well
_____ Verse 31	O)	direct his way (life path) correctly

How should knowing that God rewards people who choose the "righteous" path impact our daily choices? _____

_____

_____

_____

_____

How should knowing that God always does what is right (He is righteous) impact your confidence when you pray? _____

_____

_____

_____

_____

_____

- Notes -

_____

_____

_____

_____

_____

_____

_____

_____

_____

Read Lesson 6 Short Story: HHU Vol. 2 - Of Places and Things

- Memory Verse -

And we know that all things work together for good to those who love God, to those who are the called according to His purpose.
Romans 8:28 NASB

Approach with Reverence

Lesson 7: Worship in Spirit and in Truth

> ...unless one is born of water and the Spirit, he cannot enter the kingdom of God.

We were made for worship… each and every one of us! We are going to worship something or someone. From the very beginning God chose to walk in the Garden with Adam and Eve. They had a special time scheduled for meeting together. John 4:23 tells us that God is seeking out those who will worship Him. There is a particular kind of worshipper that He is looking for. God is looking for those whose worship will have two qualities... worship "in spirit" and worship "in truth." But what will that kind of worship look like?

Worship involves *passion*, but it isn't just passion. There are many examples of passionate worship in the Scriptures. Some of them pleased God, and some of them clearly didn't. Worship involves singing praises and adoration, but it isn't just singing. There are examples of jubilant dancing and singing in praise before the Lord and times of silence when worshippers were filled with awe and fear.

Worship will involve *prayer*, but it isn't just prayer. It seems that people are always trying to place worship into well-defined boxes that are way too small for our transcendent God. The woman at the well had been told that worshipping God was confined to a particular place (see John 4:20). Jesus blew that little box into tiny pieces. That woman was searching. She knew what everyone else was saying about how she was supposed to worship. Jesus let her know that *He* was what she had been searching for. It changed her life. **When we encounter Jesus face to face, our worship and our lives will be changed forever!**

By © Derek Ramsey / derekramsey.com. GFDL 1.2.
https://commons.wikimedia.org/w/index.php?curid=1612827

As we have already seen in Lesson 2, we must be diligent in our search for our connection with God. *What we often miss is the fact that God is also searching.* Jesus had to go through Samaria. I believe He had to go through Samaria so that He could meet with this woman who was searching for the *right way to worship God*. She was doing her part and Jesus was going to meet her there. The same will be true for each of us. We should accept the insight and understanding that others can give us in our pursuit of God, but we should never settle for anything less than a personal meeting with Jesus.

If we truly want to "worship in spirit and in truth," God will come and find us. He has already given you a treasure map that will lead you to Him. It's called the **Holy Bible**. Even better, He has provided a "Guide" who knows where the treasure can be found. **The Spirit Himself** is the guide. You can hardly go wrong when you have an infinitely perfect GPS system. The key is to listen and follow the directions. So here we go. Let's start by inviting the Holy Spirit to come and give us spiritual understanding, discernment, and wisdom. Colossians 1:9 says: *For this reason we also, since the day we heard it, do not cease to pray for you, and to ask that you may be filled with the knowledge of His will in all wisdom and spiritual understanding.*

You can't worship in spirit and truth if your spirit is dead. Ephesians 2:1,4-5 NIV tells us: *"As for you, you were dead in your transgressions and sins, but because of his great love for us, God, who is rich in mercy, made us alive with Christ even when we were dead in transgressions – it is by grace you have been saved."*

Jesus illustrated this to a Jewish religious leader (Nicodemus) by saying: *Most assuredly, I say to you, unless one is born again, he cannot see the kingdom of God. Nicodemus said to Him, How can a man be born when he is old? Can he enter a second time into his mother's womb and be born? Jesus answered, Most assuredly, I say to you, unless one is born of water and the Spirit, he cannot enter the kingdom of God. That which is born of the flesh is flesh, and that which is born of the Spirit is spirit. Do not marvel that I said to you, 'You must be born again.' The wind blows where it wishes, and you hear the sound of it, but cannot tell where it comes from and where it goes. So is everyone who is born of the Spirit. Nicodemus answered and said to Him, How can these things be? Jesus answered and said to him, Are you the teacher of Israel, and do not know these things?* John 3:3-10

That is the beginning point for understanding our worship. A corpse can't worship God (Psalm 115:17). Until our spirit is made alive by God... until we are born-again spiritually... we are a spiritual corpse. We can go through a lot of motion that makes us think we are worshipping God. Other people may think we are worshipping, but He may have a different view. The Bible has a lot to say about failed (dead) and successful (alive) attempts to worship God. **Let's take a few minutes to explore the difference between how spiritually dead people attempt to worship, and how people who are spiritually alive come to worship God.**

In **Romans chapter 12** there is a description of what acceptable worship looks like. Circle the words or phrases in this passage that represent the ambitions, attitudes or activities of a person that is spiritually alive. Just like the butterfly emerges from a cocoon, we must, with divine help, break out of our old ways, spread our wings, and fly into a new life with God.

- Living Sacrifices -

ROMANS 12:1-8 NIV

1 Therefore, I urge you, brothers, in view of God's mercy, to offer your bodies as living sacrifices, holy and pleasing to God – this is your spiritual act of worship.

2 Do not conform any longer to the pattern of this world, but be transformed by the renewing of your mind. Then you will be able to test and approve what God's will is – his good, pleasing and perfect will.

3 For by the grace given me I say to every one of you: Do not think of yourself more highly than you ought, but rather think of yourself with sober judgment, in accordance with the measure of faith God has given you.

4 Just as each of us has one body with many members, and these members do not all have the same function,

5 so in Christ we who are many form one body, and each member belongs to all the others.

6 We have different gifts, according to the grace given us. If a man's gift is prophesying, let him use it in proportion to his faith.

7 If it is serving, let him serve; if it is teaching, let him teach;

8 if it is encouraging, let him encourage; if it is contributing to the needs of others, let him give generously; if it is leadership, let him govern diligently; if it is showing mercy, let him do it cheerfully.

- LOVE -

ROMANS 12:9-21 NIV

9 Love must be sincere. Hate what is evil; cling to what is good.

10 Be devoted to one another in brotherly love. Honor one another above yourselves.

11 Never be lacking in zeal, but keep your spiritual fervor, serving the Lord.

12 Be joyful in hope, patient in affliction, faithful in prayer.

13 Share with God's people who are in need. Practice hospitality.

14 Bless those who persecute you; bless and do not curse.

15 Rejoice with those who rejoice; mourn with those who mourn.

16 Live in harmony with one another. Do not be proud, but be willing to associate with people of low position. Do not be conceited.

17 Do not repay anyone evil for evil. Be careful to do what is right in the eyes of everybody.

18 If it is possible, as far as it depends on you, live at peace with everyone.

19 Do not take revenge, my friends, but leave room for God's wrath, for it is written: "It is mine to avenge; I will repay," says the Lord.

20 On the contrary: "If your enemy is hungry, feed him; if he is thirsty, give him something to drink. In doing this, you will heap burning coals on his head."

21 Do not be overcome by evil, but overcome evil with good.

- Only God can make us born-again -

Only God can make us "born again" in our spiritual lives. When we come to Him, and invite Him to do that in our lives, we will begin to see a "transformation" in our *Ambitions, Attitudes* and *Activities*.

This is how Paul describes our lives when Christ comes in and gives us "life." 2 Corinthians 5:17 says: *Therefore, if anyone is in Christ, he is a new creation; the old has gone, the new has come!* NIV

Review the circled items from the Romans 12 passage and place them in the following categories: Ambitions, Attitudes and Activities. These are just some of the ways that God will be at work in our lives to make us truly alive and make our worship acceptable.

When God makes a person's spirit truly alive He brings transformation into our lives!		
AMBITIONS	ATTITUDES	ACTIVITIES

In the short story **Light**, Lieutenant Tim Murphy was shot down over Iraq. He was missing and presumed to be dead. Describe the kinds of feelings that his fiancé would likely have had during the two decades that he was gone and not being heard from?_____

_____

_____

Describe the feelings that she would likely have had when she heard that he had survived and was coming home. _____

_____

Describe the feelings that God has when a person is distant and separated from Him spiritually, 2 Peter 3:9, and how God might feel when that person becomes spiritually alive. Luke 15:7,10,24,32

_____

_____

Read Lesson 7 Short Story: HHU Vol. 2 - Light

- Memory Verse -

Therefore, if anyone is in Christ, he is a new creation; old things have passed away; behold, all things have become new.
2 Corinthians 5:17 **NASB**

Lesson 8: What it means to pray "In Jesus' Name"

It's about Jesus' POSITION, POWER and AUTHORITY.

Every day there are people who close a time of prayer by saying: "in Jesus' name, Amen." They might be finishing off a series of personal prayer requests, or simply thanking God for their food. Some of them know full well why they are invoking the "name of Jesus" and what that means, while others are reciting a phrase which carries very little meaning to them.

Have you ever used that phrase? What does that mean to you when you use it? _____

_____

_____

_____

_____

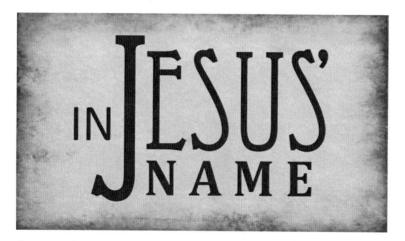

It is amazing to me how much we learn from our families through assimilation. Our family structures may look different, but we all have a unique environment that helped shape our lives. We not only learn a language, but a particular sub-set of our language that is unique to our upbringing. We share traditions, common values, shared beliefs, and a distinct history. Some of these things we treasure, and some we simply accept as the way life is supposed to be lived. In my family, finishing off any prayer with "In Jesus' name I pray, Amen" was just what was done. I had done that (and many other family practices) for many decades before I ever gave any serious thought to the depth of its meaning. That is what today's lesson seeks to explore. What does it mean to pray "In Jesus' Name"?

At some point in your life, and you are probably already there, you will sign your name to a check (or more likely) make a payment with a debit card, credit card or smart phone. When you sign (or enter a pin number), you will be telling someone that you have resources at a bank to cover the expense that you are incurring. If you don't have resources at the bank to cover the expense there will be a problem. You can sign your name to documents for a loan on a car or a house, and make an obligation to pay for what you have purchased. Over the course of time you will create a credit history that will make it easier or more difficult to obtain loans.

We can apply our experiences of "signing our name" to something to understanding what it means to **"pray in Jesus' name."**

The Bible gives us several passages that might provide some insight into this concept. When we, without permission, try to sign someone else's name to purchase something, it is called *fraud*. We can give others permission to sign their name on our behalf, which is called *Power of Attorney*. Let's begin there. How would we get permission to use Jesus' name as a means of gaining anything? Are there any limits to the ways that we can use Jesus' name in making a request?

– In Jesus' Name Matching Exercise –

In the following matching exercise, draw a line between a Bible passage and the correlating thought it expresses about things that have been, can be or will be done in response to "the name of Jesus".

Matthew 7:22	Be justified with God
John 20:31	Command demons to leave
Acts 3:16, 4:10	Exercise spiritual authority
Acts 4:30	Perform miracles
Acts 8:12	Bring good news of the Kingdom
Acts 16:18	Bring health
1 Corinthians 5:4-5	Stay away from unruly brethren
1 Corinthians 6:11	God be glorified in us
Ephesians 5:20	Believe in Him/love one another
Philippians 2:10	Signs and wonders
Colossians 3:17	Everything we do or say
2 Thessalonians 1:12	Bow our knees
2 Thessalonians 3:6	Give thanks
1 John 3:23	Have life

In the matching exercise we identified some of the things that have been, can be or will be done "in Jesus' name". We could consider those to be debits that can be made "in Jesus' Name". The next question to consider would be: Can we be confident that there are enough resources available to cover the transactions, and what right do we have to access those resources? There are three Scripture passages that might help us answer those questions. Look through these passages and select words that reveal **Jesus' POSITION** and our POSITION, **Jesus' POWER** and our POWER, and **Jesus' AUTHORITY** and our AUTHORITY.

The POSITION tab would represent the question of whether or not there is an account "in Jesus' name". Does He have a debit card that grants Him the privilege of posting transactions? Is His name on the account? A related issue would be whether or not Jesus has allowed us to have a debit card for the account, and are there any limits to our access to His account. If your parents gave you access to their checking account, and the bank asked why they should give you access to some of their resources, you might say because of our POSITION as a member of the family. *How would your resources be different if you had your own account, and only had access to money that you earned and deposited?*

The next question represented by the POWER tab could represent the question of *"how much money has been deposited?"* If you have an account balance of $5.00, you would have the "power" to access up to $5.00, but not more than that. You could probably access any amount below that, but nothing more than that amount.

The final question would be whether or not Jesus has "signing authority" for the account, and if He has given us that privilege as well. The AUTHORITY tab might be compared to whether or not the financial institution recognizes your signature or pin number as being valid. In other words: *"Do you have the authority (i.e. privilege) to make withdrawals on this account?"* How did you obtain that authority?

Select key words from these passages that represent the different tabs.

Scripture Passage	POSITION *Who holds the account?*	POWER *What's in the account?*	AUTHORITY *Why can I access the account?*
Ephesians 1:18-23			
Colossians 1:9-19			
Romans 8:16-17, 31-34, 37-39			

In preparation for the upcoming lesson find the answers to the following math questions. You can get help with this exercise, but you will need to understand the correct answers.

1. If an object travels at five feet per second, how many feet does it travel in one hour?

   [ ] A. 30   [ ] B. 300   [ ] C. 720   [ ] D. 1800   [ ] E. 18000

2. In a class of 78 students, 41 are taking French, 22 are taking German. Of the students taking French or German, 9 are taking both courses. How many students are not enrolled in either course?

   [ ] A. 6   [ ] B. 15   [ ] C. 24   [ ] D. 33   [ ] E. 54

3. A certain animal in the zoo has consumed 39 pounds of food in six days. If it continues to eat at the same rate, in how many more days will its total consumption be 91 pounds?

   [ ] A. 12   [ ] B. 11   [ ] C. 10   [ ] D. 9   [ ] E. 8

4. Sheila works 8 hours per day on Monday, Wednesday, and Friday, and 6 hours per day on Tuesday and Thursday. She does not work on Saturday and Sunday. She earns $324 per week. How much does she earn in dollars per hour?

   [ ] A. 11   [ ] B. 10   [ ] C. 9   [ ] D. 8   [ ] E. 7

5. Which of the following can be used to illustrate that not all prime numbers are odd?

   [ ] A. 1   [ ] B. 2   [ ] C. 3   [ ] D. 4   [ ] E. 5

6. A piece of ribbon 4 yards long is used to make bows requiring 15 inches of ribbon for each. What is the maximum number of bows that can be made?

   [ ] A. 8   [ ] B. 9   [ ] C. 10   [ ] D. 11   [ ] E. 12

7. The number of degrees that the hour hand of a clock moves through between noon and 2:30 in the afternoon of the same day is

   [ ] A. 720   [ ] B. 180   [ ] C. 75   [ ] D. 65   [ ] E. 60

8. Andy solves problems 74 to 125 inclusive in a Math exercise. How many problems does he solve?

   [ ] A. 53   [ ] B. 52   [ ] C. 51   [ ] D. 50   [ ] E. 49

9. 6 pints of a 20 percent solution of alcohol in water are mixed with 4 pints of a 10 percent alcohol in water solution. The percentage alcohol in the new solution is

   [ ] A. 16   [ ] B. 15   [ ] C. 14   [ ] D. 13   [ ] E. 12

10. A 3 by 4 rectangle is inscribed in circle. What is the circumference of the circle?

    [ ] A. 2.5π [ ] B. 3π [ ] C. 4π [ ] D. 5π [ ] E. 10π

- Notes -

Read Lesson 8 Short Story: HHU Vol. 2 - Drama I

- Memory Verse -

Whatever you ask in My name, that will I do, so that the Father may be glorified in the Son. If you ask Me anything in My name, I will do it. John 14:13-14 **NASB**

Lesson 9: What it doesn't mean to pray "In Jesus' Name"

"I'm 18 now and I know my rights. I can do it if I want," she said to her mother. Her father replied, "that's true, but it doesn't mean that we are no longer your parents and we have some rights as well. We have the rights that God has given us... to be honored and to have a daughter that respects the heritage that she has been given... and we also have the right to give you only those things that we believe will be good for you."

This is a fictitious conversation that has probably happened a time or two. There is sometimes a fine line

between "rights," "privileges," "expectations," and "responsibilities." At times, those lines are blurred by words like authority, independence, rules and laws. These are words that we come to both love and hate.

Some concepts, such as the laws of physics, are absolute. However, there are times when we find out that they were not as absolute as we once thought. Who knew in the 1800's that light could be bent? Once they are established as laws (at least in science) they are not likely to change. One example might be the law of gravity. If you can find your way into outer space, you may find the way gravity is impacting you in that location is different, but you haven't changed the law of gravity.

The Bill of Rights might be another good example. Every American should know the first 10 amendments that were made to the U.S. Constitution. They are known as the Bill of Rights. Let's take a look at them. **Draw a line to match the "right" in the order that they appear.**

2	Other (Fundamental or Enumerated) rights of the people.
1	Freedom from excessive bail, cruel and unusual punishments.
7	Powers reserved to the states.
8	Right of trial by jury in civil cases.
4	Right to due process of law, freedom from self-incrimination, double jeopardy.
10	Freedom from unreasonable searches and seizures.
9	Rights of accused persons, e.g., right to a speedy and public trial.
6	Right to keep and bear arms in order to maintain a well regulated militia.
3	Freedom of religion, speech, press, assembly, and petition.
5	No quartering of soldiers.

Chose one of these "rights" granted to you by the Constitution, and speculate as to how your life might be different if that right was taken away. If you live in a country outside the United States, you might ask one of two questions. *What are some similar ways that such rights are protected in your country?* If you can't make a correlation, you might ask, *how would your country be different if you had such rights guaranteed to every person in your country?*

In our last session we discovered our **Position**, **Power** and **Authority** when we come to God with our prayers. Those truths represent a great privilege that we have *as believers… as children of God*.

God has promised certain things to His children. 2 Peter 1:3-4 says: *"as His divine power has given to us all things that pertain to life and godliness, through the knowledge of Him who called us by glory and virtue, by which have been given to us exceedingly great and precious promises, that through these you may be partakers of the divine nature, having escaped the corruption that is in the world through lust."*

God always keeps His promises. Based upon His character, we have the "right" or "privilege" to ask for those things in prayer. **Look up the following Scriptures and fill in the blanks to discover how such rights might influence your prayer requests.** Verses are from the New King James version.

The right to become a child of God when we receive Him

John 1:12 But as many as _____ Him, to them He gave the _____ to become _____ of God, to those who _____ in His name.

Acts 2:21 And it shall come to pass *that* _____ calls on the name of the Lord shall be _____.

Romans 10:13 For "whoever _____ on the name of the Lord shall be _____."

The right to receive the Holy Spirit

Luke 24:49 Behold, I _____ the _____ of My Father upon you; but tarry in the city of Jerusalem until you are _____ with _____ from on high."

Acts 2:33, 38-39 Therefore being exalted to the right hand of God, and having _____ from the Father the _____ of the Holy Spirit, He poured out this which you now see and hear. Then Peter said to them, "Repent, and let every one of you be baptized in the name of Jesus Christ for the remission of sins; and you shall _____ the _____ of the _____ _____. For the _____ is to _____ and to _____ _____, and to all who are afar off, as many as the Lord our God will call."

Galatians 3:14 that the blessing of Abraham might come upon the Gentiles in Christ Jesus, that we might _____ the _____ of the _____ through faith.

The right to ask God for wisdom

James 1:5 If any of you lacks _____, let him _____ of God, who gives to all liberally and without reproach, and it will be _____ to him.

Colossians 1:9 For this reason we also, since the day we heard it, do not cease to _____ for you, and to _____ that you may be _____ with the knowledge of His will in all _____ and _____ _____;

Ephesians 1:16-17 do not cease to give thanks for you, making mention of you in my _____: that the God of our Lord Jesus Christ, the Father of glory, may _____ to you the _____ of _____ and _____ in the _____ of _____,

The right to ask forgiveness for our sins

1 John 1:9 _____ we _____ our sins, He is _____ and _____ to _____ us *our* _____ and to _____ _____ from all unrighteousness.

1 John 2:12 I write to you, little children, because your _____ are _____ you for His name's sake.

Titus 2:11-14 For the grace of God that brings _____ has appeared to all men, teaching us that, denying ungodliness and worldly lusts, we should live soberly, righteously, and godly in the present age, looking for the blessed hope and glorious appearing of our great God and Savior Jesus Christ, who gave Himself for us, that He might _____ _____ from every _____ _____ and _____ for Himself *His* own special people, _____ for _____ _____.

Acts 26:18 to open their eyes, in order to _____ _____ from _____ to _____, and from the power of _____ _____ _____, that they may receive _____ of _____ and an inheritance among those who are sanctified by faith in Me.'

The right to ask for protection from the Evil One

Matthew 6:13 And do not lead us into temptation, but _____ _____ from the _____ _____. For _____ is the kingdom and the power and the glory forever. Amen.

2 Thessalonians 3:3 But the Lord is faithful, who will _____ you and _____ you from the _____ _____.

Ephesians 6:16 above all, taking the _____ of faith with which you will be able to _____ all the fiery darts of the _____ _____.

The right to pray for guidance from God

Psalm 32:8 I will _____ you and _____ you in the way you should go; I will _____ you with My eye.

Proverbs 3:5-6 Trust in the Lord with all your heart, and lean not on your own understanding; in all your ways acknowledge Him, And _____ shall _____ your _____.

John 16:13 However, when He, the Spirit of truth, has come, He will _____ you into all _____; for He will not speak on His own authority, but whatever He hears He will speak; and He will tell you things to come.

The right to ask for the provision for our daily needs

Matthew 6:11 _____ us this day our _____ _____.

Philippians 4:19 And my God shall _____ all your _____ according to His riches in glory by Christ Jesus.

Psalm 84:11 For the Lord God *is* a sun and shield; the Lord will give grace and glory; No _____ _____ will He _____ from those who walk uprightly.

The right to reap what we sow

Galatians 6:7 Do not be _____, God is not _____; for whatever a man _____, that he will also _____.

Psalm 126:5 Those who _____ in tears shall _____ in joy.

Job 4:6 Is not your _____ your _____? And the _____ of your ways your _____?

Hosea 10:12 _____ for yourselves _____; _____ in _____; break up your fallow ground, for it is time to seek the Lord, till He comes and _____ _____ on you.

The right to pray that God the Father will bring people to saving faith

John 6:44-45 No one can come to Me _____ the Father who sent Me _____ _____; and I will raise him up at the last day. It is written in the prophets, 'And they shall all be taught by God.' Therefore everyone who has _____ and _____ from the _____ comes to _____.

Luke 10:2 Then He said to them, The harvest truly is great, but the laborers are few; therefore _____ the _____ of the harvest to _____ _____ _____ into His harvest.

Romans 10:1 Brethren, my heart's desire and _____ to _____ for Israel is that they may be _____.

From the Prayer Prompt homework, find the Scripture verse that corresponds to the following prompt. If we understand the nature of the requests and the heart we should have as we bring them, we have freedom to ask for anything. It's not a matter of measuring up to God's standards, but understanding that there are inappropriate ways and attitudes in making requests before the throne of God. Because of what Jesus has provided for us and is producing in us, we are invited to bring our requests with confidence. _____

The right to ask God's help in living a victorious, abundant life

Zephaniah 3:17   The Lord your God in your midst, the Mighty One, will save; He will _____ over _____ with _____, He will _____ _____ with His _____, He will _____ over _____ with _____."

John 10:10   The thief does not come except to steal, and to kill, and to destroy. I have _____ that they may have _____, and that they may have *it* more _____.

1 Corinthians 15:57   But thanks *be* to God, who _____ us the _____ through our Lord Jesus Christ.

1 John 5:4   For whatever is born of God overcomes the world. And this is the _____ that has _____ the world – our _____.

The right to believe that God will hear and respond to our prayers

Matthew 7:7-8, 11   _____, and it will be _____ to you; _____, and you will _____; _____, and it will be _____ to you. For everyone who asks _____, and he who seeks _____, and to him who knocks it will be _____. If you then, being evil, know how to give good gifts to your children, how _____ _____ will your Father who is in heaven give _____ _____ to those who _____ Him!

Luke 18:1, 7   Then He spoke a parable to them, that men _____ ought to _____ and not lose heart, And shall God not _____ His own elect who cry out day and night to Him, though He bears long with them?

1 John 5:14-15   Now this is the _____ that we have in Him, that if we _____ anything _____ to His will, He hears us. And if we know that He hears us, whatever we ask, we know that we _____ the _____ that we have asked of Him.

Teach Us To Pray I © 2019 I Prayerful Publishing Inc. I www.prayerfulpublishing.com I All Rights Reserved

We have the right to believe that there will be a reward for righteousness (may be in this life or in heaven)

Matthew 10:41-42   He who receives a prophet in the name of a prophet shall receive a prophet's _____. And he who receives a righteous man in the name of a righteous man shall receive a righteous man's _____. And whoever gives one of these little ones only a cup of cold water in the name of a disciple, assuredly, I say to you, he shall by no means lose his _____."

Mark 10:28-31   Then Peter began to say to Him, "See, we have left all and followed You." So Jesus answered and said, "Assuredly, I say to you, there is no one who has left house or brothers or sisters or father or mother or wife or children or lands, for My sake and the gospel's, who shall not receive a _____ _____ in this _____ – houses and brothers and sisters and mothers and children and lands, with persecutions – and in the _____ _____ _____, eternal life. But many who are first will be last, and the last first."

Psalms 58:11   So that men will say, "Surely there is a _____ for the righteous; surely He is God who _____ in the _____."

Revelation 22:12   "And behold, I am coming quickly, and My _____ is with Me, to give to every one _____ to his work.

We have the right to believe that Jesus will return to take us to live with Him

John 14:2-3   In My Father's house are many mansions; if it were not so, I would have told you. I go to prepare a place for you. And if I go and prepare a place for you, I will _____ _____ and receive you to Myself; that where _____ _____, *there* _____ _____ _____ _____.

2 Peter 3:4, 9   and saying, "Where is the _____ of His _____? For since the fathers fell asleep, all things continue as they were from the beginning of creation." The Lord is not slack concerning His _____, as some count slackness, but is longsuffering toward us, not willing that any should perish but that all should come to repentance.

1 Thessalonians 4:16-18   For the Lord Himself will _____ from heaven with a shout, with the voice of an archangel, and with the trumpet of God. And the dead in Christ will rise first. Then we who are alive *and* remain shall be _____ _____ together with them in the clouds to _____ the _____ in the _____. And thus we shall _____ be with the Lord. Therefore comfort one another with these words.

Knowing your rights as a citizen of a country, or as a Christian in God's kingdom, is vitally important. *But it is also critical that we properly understand how they can and should be applied in our lives.* Examples abound of people holding differing opinions about what the application of our rights should look like. The Supreme Court often has to give a ruling to resolve the differences of opinion.

In the Christian realm, there are significant differences about the application of our rights as well. Ultimately, the Holy Spirit giving us discernment, insight, and understanding of the Scriptures will be the final arbiter in our resolving the proper view of the application of our rights. Let's take a moment right now to ask the Holy Spirit to guide us as we consider the correct application of the promises that God has made to us.

We started this lesson with a fictitious conversation between an 18-year-old and her parents. That limited conversation illustrates how there can be differing perspectives about the expectations that we can bring into our relationships. Those expectations often hold right and wrong assumptions about each person's "rights".

Let's take a brief look at some of the assumptions that could flow out of the rights that Christians have based on the promises of God. A good example would be the way people assume that they will get whatever they ask for in Jesus' name. **Match the Prayer Prompt with the associated Scripture passage to discover the conditions that apply to getting whatever you ask for in Jesus' name.**

_____ #1	If you abide in me and my words abide in you.	A) 1 John 3:21-22
_____ #2	If our hearts don't condemn us because we obey His commands and do what pleases him.	B) John 14:13
_____ #3	If our requests are according to His will.	C) Matthew 21:22
_____ #4	So that the Son may bring glory to the Father.	D) John 15:7
_____ #5	Ask In my name…	E) 1 John 5:14
_____ #6	If you believe	F) John 14:14

 **Read Lesson 9 Short Story: HHU Vol. 2 - Drama II**

- Memory Verse -

Let us therefore come boldly to the throne of grace, that we may obtain mercy and find grace to help in time of need.
Hebrews 4:16 NASB

Approach with Reverence

Lesson 10: What it means to pray "In the Spirit"

"Son, I'm not sure that I should let you drive this car. It has 580 horsepower and I'm not sure that you can truly handle that kind of power." "Dad! you worry too much. For some reason you think that a 2015 Camaro is fine in your hands, but not in mine. If you were asking me… I would say that my reflexes are younger and quicker than yours and my eyes are better."

"That might be true, but how many times have you had to respond to crisis situations while driving a car? You may have better reflexes, but I have more experience." "So… what you are saying is that you've been in bad situations while driving more often than I have, and that makes you more qualified to deal with trouble. I would say that so far I've been able to avoid trouble while driving, which actually means that I have a safer driving record. Now hand over the keys."

"Son, I think that you are making a fallacious argument. It's not a matter of reflexes, but a matter of wisdom. It's not a matter of how quickly you can respond, but rather a matter of knowledge. Your eyes may be clearer, but the wisdom of experience will enable me to see the potential dangers before you would recognize their approach."

In this lesson we are taking a look at what it means to *pray in the Spirit*. Scripture challenges us to do just that, and we would never be asked to do something that is impossible. If God expects us to "pray in the spirit," it is reasonable to assume that He will both show us the way and help us get there.

Picture our access to God in prayer as if we have been given the keys to the aforementioned 2015 Camaro. It feels good to have access to the power and maneuverability of this amazing car. You may not know what 0-60 mph in under 4 seconds feels like, but you are about to find out. The question being raised would be, "Should you welcome some advice before you get behind the wheel for the first time?" A self-confident person might say "I can handle this – just clear the road!" A cautious person might say, "Can I start my driving lessons with a Crown Victoria and a seasoned driver training instructor?" Are there some things that you might want to know before you take to the road? Here are some possible examples.

How does a vehicle handle when braking? How does a vehicle handle when accelerating? How does a vehicle handle during a sharp turn? How does a vehicle handle when attempting to turn under slick conditions? What one safety precaution will statistically prevent three accidents over the course of an average lifetime?

When looking for answers to these and other questions about driving, would you want the advice of an official driver's instructor, your best friend, or your younger brother? Why? Once you have found your driving instructor, you will need to listen to them and follow their instructions. You will be behind the steering wheel, foot on the accelerator and brakes, but their counsel will be an invaluable part to your future success as a driver.

The same will be true in your prayer life. God has invited you to come boldly before His throne and present your requests, but you will need some guidance to become truly effective in the process. "Praying in the Spirit" will be a key that starts the motor in your prayer vehicle. If we see the Holy Spirit as our driving instructor for our prayer journey, how will we respond to His counsel, and what will the Spirit teach us as we travel along?

What will the Holy Spirit do?

Scripture records that the Holy Spirit is our helper – driver's instructor if you will. Listed below are some of the things that the Holy Spirit will do for us or in us. Each proposition has three supporting Scripture verses or passages. **In each category, rank the most significant verse in support of the premise.** 1 represents the strongest support of the premise and 3 the least supportive. In the space provided write down why you chose that one as your #1 ranking. Scripture verses are from the New King James version unless otherwise indicated.

The Holy Spirit will testify about the things of Jesus.

_____ **John 16:14-15** He will glorify Me, for He will take of what is Mine and declare it to you. All things that the Father has are Mine. Therefore I said that He will take of Mine and declare it to you.

_____ **John 15:26** But when the Helper comes, whom I shall send to you from the Father, the Spirit of truth who proceeds from the Father, He will testify of Me.

_____ **1 Corinthians 2:11-12** For what man knows the things of a man except the spirit of the man which is in him? Even so no one knows the things of God except the Spirit of God. Now we have received, not the spirit of the world, but the Spirit who is from God, that we might know the things that have been freely given to us by God.

Why was that verse chosen as the #1 support of the premise? _____

_____

_____

_____

The Holy Spirit will convict the world of sin, righteousness and justice.

_____ **John 16:8** And when He has come, He will convict the world of sin, and of righteousness, and of judgment:

_____ **John 16:9** of sin, because they do not believe in Me;

_____ **John 16:10** of righteousness, because I go to My Father and you see Me no more;

_____ **John 16:11** of judgment, because the ruler of this world is judged.

Why was that verse chosen as the #1 support of the premise? _____

_____

_____

_____

The Holy Spirit will guide you into all truth.

_____ **John 14:26** But the Helper, the Holy Spirit, whom the Father will send in My name, He will teach you all things, and bring to your remembrance all things that I said to you.

_____ **John 16:13** However, when He, the Spirit of truth, has come, He will guide you into all truth; for He will not speak on His own authority, but whatever He hears He will speak; and He will tell you things to come.

_____ **1 Corinthians 2:10, 13-14** But God has revealed them to us through His Spirit. For the Spirit searches all things, yes, the deep things of God. These things we also speak, not in words which man's wisdom teaches but which the Holy Spirit teaches, comparing spiritual things with spiritual. But the natural man does not receive the things of the Spirit of God, for they are foolishness to him; nor can he know them, because they are spiritually discerned.

Why was that verse chosen as the #1 support of the premise? _____

_____

_____

_____

The Holy Spirit will strengthen and help you.

_____ **John 14:16** And I will pray the Father, and He will give you another Helper, that He may abide with you forever —

_____ **John 16:7** Nevertheless I tell you the truth. It is to your advantage that I go away; for if I do not go away, the Helper will not come to you; but if I depart, I will send Him to you.

_____ **Isaiah 11:2 NASB** The Spirit of the LORD will rest on Him, the spirit of wisdom and understanding, the spirit of counsel and strength, The spirit of knowledge and the fear of the LORD.

Why was that verse chosen as the #1 support of the premise? _____

_____

_____

_____

> _**You have to invite the Holy Spirit to help you in all these areas and cooperate with His work in your life.**_ The Holy Spirit will be there for you each step of the way: helping you avoid danger, encouraging you to develop good driving habits, and explaining the rules of the road. His desire isn't to take away the joy of driving, but to make your driving experience more complete and fulfilling. You can welcome His involvement or ignore it. The choice is truly yours, and the rewards or consequences are yours as well.
>
> _**How should that affect your approach to your prayer life?**_

The Holy Spirit will intercede for you.

_____ **Romans 8:26** Likewise the Spirit also helps in our weaknesses. For we do not know what we should pray for as we ought, but the Spirit Himself makes intercession for us with groaning which cannot be uttered.

_____ **Romans 8:27** Now He who searches the hearts knows what the mind of the Spirit is, because He makes intercession for the saints according to the will of God.

_____ **Romans 8:34** Who is he who condemns? It is Christ who died, and furthermore is also risen, who is even at the right hand of God, who also makes intercession for us.

Why was that verse chosen as the #1 support of the premise? _____

_____

_____

_____

The Holy Spirit will protect you from the evil one.

_____ **1 John 5:18** We know that whoever is born of God does not sin; but he who has been born of God keeps himself, and the wicked one does not touch him.

_____ **2 Thessalonians 3:3** But the Lord is faithful, who will establish you and guard you from the evil one.

_____ **1 John 4:4** You are of God, little children, and have overcome them, because He who is in you is greater than he who is in the world.

Why was that verse chosen as the #1 support of the premise? _____

_____

_____

_____

The Holy Spirit will help you know how to pray.

_____ **Romans 8:26** Likewise the Spirit also helps in our weaknesses. For we do not know what we should pray for as we ought, but the Spirit Himself makes intercession for us with roaning which cannot be uttered.

_____ **Ephesians 6:18** praying always with all prayer and supplication in the Spirit, being watchful to this end with all perseverance and supplication for all the saints--

_____ **1 John 2:27** But the anointing which you have received from Him abides in you, and you do not need that anyone teach you; but as the same anointing teaches you concerning all things, and is true, and is not a lie, and just as it has taught you, you will abide in Him.

Why was that verse chosen as the #1 support of the premise? _____

_____

_____

_____

Teach Us To Pray I © 2019 I Prayerful Publishing Inc. I www.prayerfulpublishing.com I All Rights Reserved

The Holy Spirit will give you power to live a new life.

_____ **Acts 1:8** But you shall receive power when the Holy Spirit has come upon you; and you shall be witnesses to Me in Jerusalem, and in all Judea and Samaria, and to the end of the earth."

_____ **Romans 8:11** But if the Spirit of Him who raised Jesus from the dead dwells in you, He who raised Christ from the dead will also give life to your mortal bodies through His Spirit who dwells in you.

_____ **Ephesians 3:16** that He would grant you, according to the riches of His glory, to be strengthened with might through His Spirit in the inner man,

Why was that verse chosen as the #1 support of the premise? _____

_____

_____

_____

The Holy Spirit will transform you.

_____ **Ephesians 5:18** And do not be drunk with wine, in which is dissipation; but be filled with the Spirit,

_____ **Titus 3:5-6** not by works of righteousness which we have done, but according to His mercy He saved us, through the washing of regeneration and renewing of the Holy Spirit, whom He poured out on us abundantly through Jesus Christ our Savior,

_____ **Romans 12:1-2** I beseech you therefore, brethren, by the mercies of God, that you present your bodies a living sacrifice, holy, acceptable to God, which is your reasonable service. And do not be conformed to this world, but be transformed by the renewing of your mind, that you may prove what is that good and acceptable and perfect will of God

Why was that verse chosen as the #1 support of the premise? _____

_____

_____

_____

The Holy Spirit will make all things new.

_____ **2 Corinthians 5:17** Therefore, if anyone is in Christ, he is a new creation; old things have passed away; behold, all things have become new

_____ **2 Peter 1:4** by which have been given to us exceedingly great and precious promises, that through these you may be partakers of the divine nature, having escaped the corruption that is in the world through lust.

_____ **Romans 7:6** But now we have been delivered from the law, having died to what we were held by, so that we should serve in the newness of the Spirit and not in the oldness of the letter.

Why was that verse chosen as the #1 support of the premise? _____

_____

_____

_____

The Holy Spirit will create new qualities in your life.

_____ **Galatians 5:22-23** But the fruit of the Spirit is love, joy, peace, longsuffering, kindness, goodness, faithfulness, gentleness, self-control. Against such there is no law.

_____ **2 Peter 1:2-3** Grace and peace be multiplied to you in the knowledge of God and of Jesus our Lord, as His divine power has given to us all things that pertain to life and godliness, through the knowledge of Him who called us by glory and virtue,

_____ **Romans 15:13** Now may the God of hope fill you with all joy and peace in believing, that you may abound in hope by the power of the Holy Spirit.

Why was that verse chosen as the #1 support of the premise? _____

_____

_____

_____

_____

- Notes -

_____

_____

_____

_____

_____

_____

_____

_____

Read Lesson 10 Short Story: HHU Vol. 1 - Reluctant Hero

- Memory Verse -

Likewise the Spirit also helps in our weaknesses. For we do not know what we should pray for as we ought, but the Spirit Himself makes intercession for us with groanings which cannot be uttered.
Romans 8:26 **NKJV**

Approach with Reverence

Lesson 11: What it doesn't mean to pray "In the Spirit"

There were many leaders in the civil rights movement of the 1960s. Dr. Martin Luther King became known as the leader of that movement because of the power of his words and the strength of his convictions.

There were phrases shared that had the power to change a nation's consciousness. Phrases like *"I have a dream that my four little children will one day live in a nation where they will not be judged by the color of their skin but by the content of their character."* There was that "special something" about the words that flowed from this man and the heart that prompted those words. It is the "that's it" quality that is nearly indefinable, but you know it when you see it and hear it. One wishes that they could measure it, define it and pass it on to others, but that seems to be beyond us. When it comes to praying in the Spirit or not, you might find yourself in a similar position.

The Spirit of God cannot be manipulated, marketed or manhandled. There is no need for or benefit to defining what praying in the Spirit is or is not. As Yoda said *"There is no try... there is only do or do not."* As we look at what praying in the Spirit is like and what it is not like, we will not attempt to reduce it to a formula or something which we strive to accomplish. To do so would be to place boundaries on and definitions to the work of the infinite God. Our goal is not to define this calling from God, but to encourage ourselves to embrace it. We will attempt to bring to light what God has clearly instructed us to do "to pray in the spirit"... and to avoid any attempts to counterfeit its place in our lives.

In our attempt to discover what "praying in the Spirit" will look like and/or not look like, we will observe what happened when the church began. After the coming of the Holy Spirit, the church took on certain characteristics and qualities. While the beginnings were at times confusing and chaotic, it does point us in the direction of what God might desire for the church. So let's do a little searching in two categories (prayer and the work of the Holy Spirit in the book of Acts) to see what "praying in the Spirit" might entail. What are your observations of the **work of the Holy Spirit** in the early church in each chapter? How was **prayer** a part of the early church in each chapter?

What do you observe about the work of the Holy Spirit in the early church from Acts chapter 1? _____

_____

_____

_____

_____

What do you observe about prayer in the early church from chapter 1? _____

_____

_____

_____

What do you observe about the work of the Holy Spirit in the early church from Acts chapter 2? _____

_____

_____

_____

What do you observe about prayer in the early church from chapter 2? _____

_____

_____

_____

What do you observe about the work of the Holy Spirit in the early church from Acts chapter 3? _____

_____

_____

_____

What do you observe about prayer in the early church from chapter 3? _____

_____

_____

_____

What do you observe about the work of the Holy Spirit in the early church from Acts chapter 4? _____

_____

_____

_____

What do you observe about prayer in the early church from chapter 4? _____

_____

_____

_____

What do you observe about the work of the Holy Spirit in the early church from Acts chapter 6? _____

_____

_____

_____

What do you observe about prayer in the early church from chapter 6? _____

_____

_____

_____

What do you observe about the work of the Holy Spirit in the early church from Acts chapter 8? _____

_____

_____

_____

What do you observe about prayer in the early church from chapter 8? _____

_____

_____

_____

What do you observe about the work of the Holy Spirit in the early church from Acts chapter 9? _____

_____

_____

_____

What do you observe about prayer in the early church from chapter 9? _____

_____

_____

_____

What do you observe about the work of the Holy Spirit in the early church from Acts chapter 10 & 11? _____

_____

_____

_____

What do you observe about prayer in the early church from chapter 10 & 11? _____

_____

_____

_____

What do you observe about the work of the Holy Spirit in the early church from Acts chapter 12? _____

_____

_____

_____

What do you observe about prayer in the early church from chapter 12? _____

_____

_____

_____

What do you observe about the work of the Holy Spirit in the early church from Acts chapter 13? _____

_____

_____

_____

What do you observe about prayer in the early church from chapter 13? _____

_____

_____

_____

What do you observe about the work of the Holy Spirit in the early church from Acts chapter 14? _____

_____

_____

_____

What do you observe about prayer in the early church from chapter 14? _____

_____

_____

_____

What do you observe about the work of the Holy Spirit in the early church from Acts chapter 16? _____

_____

_____

_____

What do you observe about prayer in the early church from chapter 16? _____

_____

_____

_____

What do you observe about the work of the Holy Spirit in the early church from Acts chapter 22? _____

_____

_____

_____

What do you observe about prayer in the early church from chapter 22? _____

_____

_____

Review the various observations about the work of the Holy Spirit and the place of prayer in the early church, and record these observations in a summary statement. _____

_____

_____

_____

_____

_____

_____

- Notes -

_____

_____

_____

_____

_____

Read Lesson 11 Short Story: HHU Vol. 2 - Premonition

- Memory Verse -

The man without the Spirit does not accept the things that come from the Spirit of God, for they are foolishness to him, and he cannot understand them, because they are spiritually discerned.

1 Corinthians 2:14 **NIV**

Approach with Reverence

Lesson 12: What it means to pray "in Truth"

Prayer changes things!

You have probably heard someone say that "Prayer Changes Things" and wondered if that could really be true. We have now had eleven lessons that were designed to help you in your connection with God. If you aren't yet convinced that "your prayers can actually change things," then it's time to once again look at the examples provided by some of the people who really knew how to connect with God. We will look into God's Word and pull up some of the passages that include the words "I pray" or "my prayer."

Write the name of the person who most likely prayed those words, and what difference you believe it made in their world. Some of these are very straightforward (i.e. their name is actually given) and some a little more difficult. Feel free to invite someone you trust to help you figure out the answers. One of the simplest ways to find out who said it would be to read the verses just before and those just after what was being referenced. Here's another good hint. Look at the particular book of the Bible it is taken from as your first hint. Unless otherwise indicated, all Scripture passages are taken from the New King James Version. *Happy Hunting!*

I pray.....   My prayer.....

Genesis 32:29 Then Jacob asked, saying, "Tell me Your name, **I pray**." And He said, "Why is it that you ask about My name?" And He blessed him there. ***Who said it?*** _____
What difference did it make? _____
_____
_____

Exodus 33:13 Now therefore, **I pray**, if I have found grace in Your sight, show me now Your way, that I may know You and that I may find grace in Your sight. And consider that this nation is Your people.
Who said it? _____ ***What difference did it make?*** _____
_____
_____

Exodus 33:18 NASB Then Moses said, "**I pray** You, show me Your glory!"
Who said it? _____ ***What difference did it make?*** _____
_____
_____

Numbers 12:13   So Moses cried out to the Lord, saying, "Please heal her, O God, **I pray**!"

Who said it? _____   *What difference did it make?* _____

_____

Numbers 14:17,19   "And now, **I pray**, let the power of my Lord be great, just as You have spoken, saying, Pardon the iniquity of this people, **I pray**, according to the greatness of Your mercy, just as You have forgiven this people, from Egypt even until now." *Who said it?* _____   *What difference did it make?* _____

_____

Deuteronomy 3:25   **I pray**, let me cross over and see the good land beyond the Jordan, those pleasant mountains, and Lebanon. *Who said it?* _____   *What difference did it make?* _____

_____

_____

Judges 6:18   "Do not depart from here, **I pray**, until I come to You and bring out my offering and set it before You." And He said, "I will wait until you come back." *Who said it?* _____

What difference did it make? _____

_____

_____

1 Samuel 23:11   "Will the men of Keilah deliver me into his hand? Will Saul come down, as Your servant has heard? O Lord God of Israel, **I pray**, tell Your servant." And the Lord said, "He will come down."

Who said it? _____   *What difference did it make?* _____

_____

_____

2 Samuel 15:31   Then someone told David, saying, "Ahithophel is among the conspirators with Absalom." And David said, "O Lord, **I pray**, turn the counsel of Ahithophel into foolishness!" *Who said it?* _____

What difference did it make? _____

_____

_____

1 Kings 8:26   And now **I pray**, O God of Israel, let Your word come true, which You have spoken to Your servant David my father *Who said it?* _____   *What difference did it make?* _____

_____

_____

1 Kings 17:21 And he stretched himself out on the child three times, and cried out to the Lord and said, "O Lord my God, **I pray**, let this child's soul come back to him." ***Who said it?*** _____

What difference did it make? _____

_____

2 Kings 6:17,18 And Elisha prayed, and said, "Lord, **I pray**, open his eyes that he may see." Then the Lord opened the eyes of the young man, and he saw. And behold, the mountain was full of horses and chariots of fire all around Elisha. So when the Syrians came down to him, Elisha prayed to the Lord, and said, "Strike this people, **I pray**, with blindness." And He struck them with blindness according to the word of Elisha.

Who said it? _____   ***What difference did it make?*** _____

_____

_____

_____

2 Kings 19:19 "Now therefore, O Lord our God, **I pray**, save us from his hand, that all the kingdoms of the earth may know that You are the Lord God, You alone." ***Who said it?*** _____

What difference did it make? _____

_____

_____

2 Chronicles 6:40 "Now, my God, **I pray**, let Your eyes be open and let Your ears be attentive to the prayer made in this place." ***Who said it?*** _____   ***What difference did it make?*** _____

_____

_____

_____

Nehemiah 1:5-11 NKJV And I said: "**I pray**, Lord God of heaven, O great and awesome God, You who keep Your covenant and mercy with those who love You and observe Your commandments, please let Your ear be attentive and Your eyes open, that You may hear the prayer of Your servant which **I pray** before You now, day and night, for the children of Israel Your servants, and confess the sins of the children of Israel which we have sinned against You. Both my father's house and I have sinned. We have acted very corruptly against You, and have not kept the commandments, the statutes, nor the ordinances which You commanded Your servant Moses. Remember, **I pray**, the word that You commanded Your servant Moses, saying, 'If you are unfaithful, I will scatter you among the nations; but if you return to Me, and keep My commandments and do them, though some of you were cast out to the farthest part of the heavens, yet I will gather them from there, and bring them to the place which I have chosen as a dwelling for My name.' Now these are Your servants and Your people, whom You have redeemed by Your great power, and by Your strong hand. O Lord, **I pray**, please let Your ear be attentive to the prayer of Your servant, and to the prayer of Your servants who desire to fear Your name; and let Your servant prosper this day, **I pray**, and grant him mercy in the sight of this man." For I was the king's cupbearer. ***Who said it?*** _____

What difference did it make? _____

_____

_____

Job 10:9   Remember, **I pray**, that You have made me like clay. And will You turn me into dust again?

Who said it? _____   *What difference did it make?* _____

_____

Job 16:17   Although no violence is in my hands, And **my prayer** is pure.

Who said it? _____   *What difference did it make?* _____

_____

_____

Psalms 5:2   Give heed to the voice of my cry, My King and my God, For to You **I will pray**.

Who said it? _____   *What difference did it make?* _____

_____

_____

Psalms 39:12   "Hear **my prayer**, O Lord, And give ear to my cry; Do not be silent at my tears; For I am a stranger with You, A sojourner, as all my fathers were." *Who said it?* _____

What difference did it make? _____

_____

_____

_____

Psalms 66:19   But certainly God has heard me; He has attended to the voice of **my prayer**.

Who said it? _____   *What difference did it make?* _____

_____

_____

Psalms 69:13   But as for me, **my prayer** is to You, O Lord, in the acceptable time; O God, in the multitude of Your mercy, Hear me in the truth of Your salvation. *Who said it?* _____

What difference did it make? _____

_____

_____

Psalm 118:25   Save now, **I pray**, O Lord; O Lord, **I pray**, send now prosperity

Who said it? _____   *What difference did it make?* _____

_____

_____

_____

Psalm 119:76, 108   Let, **I pray**, Your merciful kindness be for my comfort, According to Your word to Your servant Accept, **I pray**, the freewill offerings of my mouth, O Lord, And teach me Your judgments,

Who said it? _____   *What difference did it make?* _____

_____

_____

Psalm 141:2,5   Let **my prayer** be set before You as incense, The lifting up of my hands as the evening sacrifice. Let the righteous strike me; It shall be a kindness. And let him rebuke me; It shall be as excellent oil; Let my head not refuse it. For still **my prayer** is against the deeds of the wicked.

Who said it? _____   *What difference did it make?* _____

_____

_____

Lamentations 3:56 NASB   You have heard my voice, "Do not hide Your ear from **my prayer** for relief, From my cry for help."

Who said it? _____   *What difference did it make?* _____

_____

_____

Isaiah 38:3-5   and said, "Remember now, O Lord, **I pray**, how I have walked before You in truth and with a loyal heart, and have done what is good in Your sight." And Hezekiah wept bitterly. And the word of the Lord came to Isaiah, saying, Go and tell Hezekiah, 'Thus says the Lord, the God of David your father: "I have heard your prayer, I have seen your tears; surely I will add to your days fifteen years.   *Who said it?* _____

What difference did it make? _____

_____

_____

_____

Jeremiah 29:11-13   'For I know the plans that I have for you,' declares the LORD, 'plans for welfare and not for calamity to give you a future and a hope. 'Then you will call upon Me and come and **pray to Me**, and I will listen to you. 'You will seek Me and find Me when you search for Me with all your heart.'

Who said it? _____   *What difference did it make?* _____

_____

_____

Jeremiah 42:4   Then Jeremiah the prophet said to them, "I have heard you. Behold, **I am going to pray to the LORD** your God in accordance with your words; and I will tell you the whole message which the LORD will answer you. I will not keep back a word from you."   *Who said it?* _____

What difference did it make? _____

_____

Amos 7:2 And so it was, when they had finished eating the grass of the land, that I said: "O Lord God, forgive, **I pray!** Oh, that Jacob may stand, For he is small!"

Who said it? _____ *What difference did it make?* _____

_____

_____

Jonah 2:7 "While I was fainting away, I remembered the LORD, And **my prayer** came to You, Into Your holy temple."

Who said it? _____ *What difference did it make?* _____

_____

_____

John 17:9,20,21 "**I pray** for them. I do not pray for the world but for those whom You have given Me, for they are Yours. I do not pray for these alone, but also for those who will believe in Me through their word; that they all may be one, as You, Father, are in Me, and I in You; that they also may be one in Us, that the world may believe that You sent Me."

Who said it? _____ *What difference did it make?* _____

_____

_____

Romans 10:1 NLT God knows how often **I pray** for you. Day and night I bring you and your needs in prayer to God, whom I serve with all my heart by telling others the Good News about his Son. *Who said it?* _____

What difference did it make? _____

_____

_____

Philemon 1:6 NIV **I pray** that you may be active in sharing your faith, so that you will have a full understanding of every good thing we have in Christ.

Who said it? _____ *What difference did it make?* _____

_____

_____

3 John 1:2 Beloved, **I pray** that you may prosper in all things and be in health, just as your soul prospers.

Who said it? _____ *What difference did It make?* _____

_____

_____

What difference did all these examples make in your conviction that "Prayer Changes Things?"

_____

_____

_____

Personalize Paul's Prayers

Personalize Paul's prayers by inserting your name or the appropriate pronoun in the following blanks.

Ephesians 1:15-20 Therefore I also, after I heard of_____ faith in the Lord Jesus and _____ love for all the saints, I do not cease to give thanks for _____, making mention of _____ in my prayers: that the God of our Lord Jesus Christ, the Father of glory, may give to _____ the spirit of wisdom and revelation in the knowledge of Him, the eyes of _____ understanding being enlightened; that _____ may know what is the hope of His calling, what are the riches of the glory of His inheritance in the saints, and what is the exceeding greatness of His power toward _____ who believes, according to the working of His mighty power which He worked in Christ when He raised Him from the dead and seated Him at His right hand in the heavenly places.

Ephesians 3:16-18 NLT I pray that from his glorious, unlimited resources he will empower _____ with inner strength through his Spirit. Then Christ will make his home in _____ heart as _____ trusts in him. _____ roots will grow down into God's love and keep you strong. And may _____ have the power to understand, as all God's people should, how wide, how long, how high, and how deep his love is.

Philippians 1:3-11 I thank my God upon every remembrance of _____, always in every prayer of mine making request for _____ all with joy, for _____ fellowship in the gospel from the first day until now, being confident of this very thing, that He who has begun a good work in _____ will complete it until the day of Jesus Christ; just as it is right for me to think this of _____, because I have _____ in my heart, inasmuch as both in my chains and in the defense and confirmation of the gospel, _____ is a partaker with me of grace. For God is my witness, how greatly I long for _____ all with the affection of Jesus Christ. And this I pray, that _____ love may abound still more and more in knowledge and all discernment, that _____ may approve the things that are excellent, that _____ may be sincere and without offense till the day of Christ, being filled with the fruits of righteousness which are by Jesus Christ, to the glory and praise of God.

Colossians 1:9-11 For this reason we also, since the day we heard it, do not cease to pray for _____, and to ask that_____ may be filled with the knowledge of His will in all wisdom and spiritual understanding; that _____ may walk worthy of the Lord, fully pleasing Him, being fruitful in every good work and increasing in the knowledge of God; strengthened with all might, according to His glorious power, for all patience and longsuffering with joy.

Read Lesson 12 Short Story: HHU Vol. 1 - Nature of the Beast

- Memory Verse -

I pray that the eyes of your heart may be enlightened, so that you will know what is the hope of His calling, what are the riches of the glory of His inheritance in the saints. Ephesians 1:18 **NASB**

Prayer Prompts Calendar

NOW AVAILABLE for your favorite device...
FREE for Apple devices from The App Store and
FREE for Android devices at Google Play.

Providing Biblical Tools to Support Your Christian Walk

Teach us to Pray
Unit Contents: